On Being an Earth Being

On Being an Earth Being

Searching for the Spiritual in a Cosmic Sanctuary
Called Planet Earth

NORMAN C. HABEL

RESOURCE *Publications* • Eugene, Oregon

ON BEING AN EARTH BEING
Searching for the Spiritual in a Cosmic Sanctuary Called Planet Earth

Copyright © 2020 Norman C. Habel. All rights reserved. Except for brief quotations in critical publications or reviews, no part of this book may be reproduced in any manner without prior written permission from the publisher. Write: Permissions, Wipf and Stock Publishers, 199 W. 8th Ave., Suite 3, Eugene, OR 97401.

Resource Publications
An Imprint of Wipf and Stock Publishers
199 W. 8th Ave., Suite 3
Eugene, OR 97401

www.wipfandstock.com

PAPERBACK ISBN: 978-1-7252-5925-6
HARDCOVER ISBN: 978-1-7252-5926-3
EBOOK ISBN: 978-1-7252-5927-0

Manufactured in the U.S.A. 02/04/20

Contents

Preface		vii
I	My Adoption	1
II	My Heritage	15
III	My Earth Identity	25
IV	Sacrament of Ochre	35
V	My Cosmic Sanctuary	45
VI	My Wisdom Probing	59
VII	My Journey with Job	71
VIII	My Country	87
IX	My Innate Spirituality	101
X	My Double Faith	115
Conclusion: My 'Life' Line		129
Appendix A: Rite of Homecoming		139
Appendix B: Workshop: Exploring Earth Spirituality		151
Appendix C: Celebrating our Cosmic Sanctuary		155
Bibliography		167

Preface

After years of
dancing with dangerous doctrines,
evading unfriendly ecclesiastical missiles,
and
mining the ancient Hebrew text
of the Old Testament
for forgotten fossils of faith,
I have chosen to search
for the spiritual here and now
in that amazing cosmic sanctuary
called Planet Earth.

This text of this volume is
a re-write of my identity,
a retrieval of my inner consciousness
from being overtly religious
to being silently spiritual,
a resurrection of my spirituality,
a discovery of my innate wisdom
as I search for the Spiritual in a sanctuary
called Planet Earth.

PREFACE

This re-write
is also an invitation for any Earth Being
to search for Earth Spirituality with me
and the Aboriginal Peoples of Australia
and to reflect on my findings
as spiritual moments
of mystery
and wonder.

I

My Adoption

ADOPTED

Some years ago,
half listening to a baptism rite in my church,
I heard the word 'adopted'
for the first time.
Adopted! What did that mean?

In half a century, I performed hundreds of baptisms...
My first: an emergency baptism
in an old tin shed on Kangaroo Island
where the font was a rusty bucket;
a bucket baptism!

Everyone believed that
that bucket baptism
saved that baby heading to hell.

In my self-satisfied seventies,
I was confronted by the language of adoption
for the first time.

Why was I being adopted?
And who were my real parents?

CLEANSED

I was baptised at Hochkirk[1]
in the name of the
Father, Son, Holy Ghost;
the pastor, and congregation,
spoke German.

The pastor added the injunction:
'*Fahre aus du unreiniger Geist!*':
'Get out you unclean spirit!'

I was adopted,
welcomed into the family of God,
cleansed of any unclean spirit
lurking inside me—
and some of the original sin
that polluted my soul.

I was baptised:
a cleansed,
adopted,
and
happy little baby—
at least according to
Mother Church.

---

1. A small community in rural Victoria, Australia.

BAD BABY

On reflection,
I realised just what a bad baby
I was believed to be:
a bad baby,
who needed rescuing, cleansing
and adopting.

My bad beginning was traced back
to my biological father, Adam,
whose primal sin
—transferred by spiritual genes
through all generations of human
beings—
polluted my inner being,
my simple soul.

Because I was so bad,
an unclean spirit found a home in my soul
and apparently delighted in my
lack of purity.

An innocent child?
No, a very bad baby
living in Australia.

INNATE SIN

According to Mother Church
I was a bad baby:
polluted with innate sin
for the rest of my life.

Every Sunday I was taught to say:
'I, a poor miserable sinner,
confess unto thee my sins and iniquities
for which I deserve punishment
in time and eternity'.

The unclean spirit
was expunged at my baptism;
my innate sin remained;
evidence of its presence
had to be forgiven
every Sunday.

There was nothing about deep love,
innate Wisdom,
or primal goodness!

Nothing about a rich innate Spirit
rising from within,
ready to celebrate life.

Instead,
I was forced to live
with the dangerous doctrine
of Original Sin.

ADOPTIVE MOTHER

I discovered
the sacrament of baptism
was really
a rite of adoption
into the family of God
called 'the Church'.

God was now my true father
and the church my new mother,
committed to caring for me
—and my spiritual life—
in the true faith.

Yet, for most of my life,
I had never really considered
my identity prior to being baptised:
an innocent of another mother.

I knew Sylvia was
my biological human mother—
my birth mother;
who is the spiritual mother
from whom I was taken
to be adopted?
Who is my true mother?
Who am I?
Norman Charles who?

STOLEN

Just as difficult for me
was the cold realisation that
my situation
as a bad baby
was analogous
to experiences of many
Aboriginal people of this land:
removed,
stolen as children
from their families,
from their birth mothers,
'for their own good'.

In Australia
stolen children were separated:
cut off from their traditional communities,
located in institutions hundreds of miles away;
adopted into 'white' families;
until the early 1970s.

In the 1990s
a Supreme Court commission
investigated the practice
and released a damning report:
Bringing Them Home.

Was I stolen from my original mother
because I was a bad baby
polluted with the black stain—
the black shame—of original sin?

And how do I find my way home
and discover my true mother
here in Australia?

NEW BABY

According to the rite of baptism,
my adoption was a second 'birth':
when I emerged from the waters of baptism
I was a baby being 'born again'.

I was now God's child,
'born of water and the Spirit',
and my family name was 'Christian'.
I was, in the words of the hymn,
'a child and heir of heaven'.

According to the church—
my adoptive family—
I was given a cleansed soul by God;
this purged inner me was my true identity.

My body
remained a fragile abode:
my sanitised soul's temporary residence.
One day, I was told,
I would leave that body and Earth,
and return home to my eternal abode,
and to my God—
my spiritual Father who resided in heaven above.

I was now identified as a 'heaven being',
a spiritual soul housed temporarily
in a body made of matter.
I was also warned that this 'earthy body'
could easily go astray—
and then I would never find my way back
home to heaven.
I was made to feel safe and secure in my adoptive family,

with God watching over me—
and all adopted children who loved God's son, Jesus.

I was now, according to Mother Church,
stolen, cleansed,
adopted—
and safe!

What more could I ask?

ADOPTED LAMB

I remember, when I was a boy on the farm,
we would sometimes adopt a baby lamb.

The mother of the lamb died giving birth;
my father, finding the lamb on the ground,
close to death,
would bring it home and feed it.

My brother and I would adopt the lamb:
it became a member of our farm family.
It would follow us everywhere,
looking for food and friendship.
Sometimes, when the lamb became independent,
it would return to the flock.

But sometimes
it remained part of our family all its life.
Perhaps I understand now
why I used to sing:
I am Jesus' little lamb,
Therefore glad at heart I am.

I did not appreciate
the reality of the birth mother
of the lamb
on the farm
—or in church.

Perhaps I should have been singing:
'I was Jesus' little lamb;
now I wonder who I am'?

ADOPTED COSMOLOGY

In my adoptive family
I was indoctrinated to accept by faith that
the cosmos was created by God,
controlled by God,
ruled by God:
the Supreme Being above.

The cosmos was quite explicitly dual in nature:
the spiritual world of God;
the earthly world where created beings live.
The spiritual world was superior and eternal;
the material or earthly world was inferior, transitory and 'fallen'.
Yes, fallen!

God could intervene in the earthly world
if God chose—
as in the great flood
when God threatened to destroy Earth forever.

God's spiritual world was located above
in a domain called heaven—
a separate world full of angel choirs
and the departed faithful.

Many believed that it did not matter
what happened to Earth:
ultimately Earth would be eliminated
and heaven would be our real home;
or, in more popular terms:
'We are going to heaven, so to hell with Earth'.

Earth is a stopover on the road to eternity:
we were told we are strangers on Earth
desiring a 'better country' called heaven.

Earth is a 'barren land'
as the famous hymn acclaims:
Guide me O thou great Jehovah,
Pilgrim through this barren land.

And Australia
is one of the temporary stopovers
in that 'barren land', Earth.

MY FINDING

*Baptism
is a rite of adoption:
even though I was believed to be
a bad little baby,
filled with sin,
I was adopted by Mother Church
who promised to nurture me
in the true faith
as a new born
child of God
destined for heaven—
even though I lived
on Planet Earth.*

II

My Heritage

RECORDS

I began my search for my mother
by perusing the church records
for any hint of the birth mother
—from whom I was taken—
to be adopted into the family of God
and the Lutheran church.

My 'Christian name', Norman Charles:
a record and symbol of my baptism
at Hochkirk Lutheran Church in 1932;
there was no record of
my original birth mother
or her 'fallen' nature.

The Lyndoch Lutheran congregation
noted my great grandfather
sinning boldly
by going to the goldfields
rather than staying at home with the Lutherans
—and their God in exile with them—
in the Barossa Valley.

My record shows that, at 14 years of age,
I was confirmed as a true Lutheran:
permitted to wear long pants
and allowed to go to holy communion
with the men.

I had become a recognised member
of the family of God,
also known as 'Mother Church'—
in spite of my innate sin.

BIBLE

According to my adopting mother
the Lutheran church,
the Bible contains answers
to every question or crisis in life—
answers that come directly from God.

And, as far as I can recall,
the Bible was the only book
in my home back on the farm.

My Bible, I was told,
made it abundantly clear
that I was a sinner like Adam;
the only way I could be saved
from this dreadful sin
was believing in Jesus Christ
who died for my sins
on the cross.

When I began to read my Holy Bible
with the eyes of history,
science and ecology,
I was denounced as a heretic.

There lingered a dream, however,
from the memory of my great grandfather
—the tree whisperer—
that my Bible
was more than a book of answers.

In my memory dream,
my great grandfather told me that
the Holy Bible might also

be explored
as a book of mysteries
about ancient faith fossils,
about nature surrounding me,
about the Spiritual within me—
and my real identity
as an Earth being.

WISDOM TREE

One day I looked again
at the infamous myth of the Fall in Genesis;
a myth—
a colourful primal narrative,
embossed with bold poetic images,
giving cultural meaning to people.

The 'tree of the knowledge of good and evil',
in the flamboyant forest called Eden,
is not an acidic apple tree
that has the effect of polluting
the genes of humans with original sin.
It is a Wisdom tree.

As the snake revealed,
the eyes of Adam and Eve were opened
when they ate fruit from the Wisdom tree.
As soon as they tasted the fruit,
they were enlightened with Wisdom:
knowledge of good and evil;
knowledge of life in the real world, Planet Earth.

The real world of a farm boy—
as distinct from the imaginary world of Eden—
is replete with cunning snakes,
painful childbirth,
hard work,
bread and wine.

As a descendant of Adam and Eve,
I do not need to be cleansed of original sin.
I can celebrate my enlightenment,
my innate Wisdom,

my emerging consciousness of the real world
into which I was born.

What would change if I were to celebrate
my innate Wisdom
rather than rue my innate sin?

DUST MAN

A re-view of the myth about Adam and Eve
involves a serious examination
of the origin of the first man and woman
and their fate.

A close reading of the Hebrew reveals
that this primal human
was made of dust!
Yes, dust!
Red dust from the ground!

God, a specialist potter
mysteriously
transformed the red dust from the ground
into a dust figure called Adam.

When God breathed into the dust,
the figure did not blow away;
the dust was alive.

The last words God spoke to the dust-man,
after the so-called Fall,
are ominous:
'You are dust and to dust you shall return!'

Dead or alive,
Adam is dust!

So, is dust my true mother?

SOFT SOIL

As a youth,
I remember my father taking me into the dry fields
and walking slowly with him across the ground
prepared for sowing
before the rains came.

He would kneel, take a handful of soft soil,
hold it in his palms for some time,
then let it run slowly through his fingers
back to the ground.

In that moment he seemed to connect
with the very soul of the soil
as he said to himself:
'Good earth. This is good earth'.

I can still smell the rich aroma of the earth
in the furrows
turned over by a team of draught horses.

I loved the soil:
its feel,
its smell,
its colours.

As I recalled my youth on the farm,
I discovered that I had
a kinship with the red clay in Australia
—a latent link with Planet Earth as my Mother—
even if Mother Church
would not hear me.

BACK TO EDEN

As a boy
I wandered through the bush,
caressing the green moss on red gums
hundreds of years old,
tasting the soft blossom of blooming wattles,
smelling the aroma of crushed eucalyptus leaves,
hearing the sounds—my country's music—
in the air surrounding me.

Then one day,
a revelation from Mother Earth.
What I was reading about God's Spirit came to life.
I breathed, in time with the trees;
in tune with the breeze,
I inhaled deeply.

I was breathing the breath of God,
as Adam did, in the forest of Eden.

According to the Book of Genesis
the air,
the wind,
the atmosphere,
are the breath of God:
the Spiritual in Planet Earth,
the Spirit
that animated me
and every tree in every age.

I was in Eden
with a fellow Earth being
called Adam.

MY FINDING

*In the records
about my spiritual nature,
there are hints that,
in spite of church teachings
and the story of the Fall,
I have a kinship with Planet Earth—
especially in the Red Centre of Australia—
a kinship that is more than
geological.*

III

My Earth Identity

DOUBLE FAITH

After searching through the Bible,
my memory,
and the teachings of the church,
I discerned lingering features in my faith
that might be the heresy of
double faith.

I researched the history of my great-grandfather,
a Wend from Prussia:
one of the forest people
who came to Australia in the early 1850s.
The Wends were accused of double faith:
they went to church on Sunday
and acknowledged Jesus Christ;
during the week,
they connected with the life-forces of Nature,
and blessed Mother Earth
to ensure a healthy harvest
and a fertile future.

I identified my great father as a
tree whisperer.
I began to wonder whether I too
had a double faith,
that I was really an Earth whisperer:
a land whisperer,
living in Australia.

HIDDEN TEXT

I discovered a forgotten fossil:
a Bible text that seems to be
a church secret;
a text that suggests the psalmist
is proclaiming a double faith.

After proclaiming that the Spirit
is everywhere,
from the highest heavens
to the bed of the underworld,
the psalmist announces:
I am actually made *in secret,*
intricately formed
in the depths of Earth![2]

The psalmist is confessing
to being an embryo
delicately formed in Earth,
that Planet Earth is the mother,
of every Earth child!

For me,
the secret was out!
I was not the first to contemplate
that Earth was my Mother,
that I was
an Earth child.

---

2. See Psalm 139:13–15.

ECOLOGY

Then came the big surprise—
a new insight:
a last minute revelation
to a tired old prophet
waiting in the wings of Wisdom.

The word-seen-new was 'ecology'.

I had considered
ecology
just another science,
complementing biology, physics and psychology.

No!
ecology,
I discovered, is a new worldview:
a challenging cosmology making Galileo cringe;
a consciousness revolution!

Some compare ecology with a cosmic web
where everything is connected—
and there's no sacred spider.
Some speak of a whirlpool
of animate and inanimate forces
bouncing and balancing, flourishing
in the wind of time.

Ecology means
everything is inter-connected
and related
socially, biologically
and spiritually!

And Planet Earth?
Planet Earth is a wondrous womb:
land forces and life forces
combining to create new lives,
new mysteries, new wonders;
Planet Earth is a cosmic sanctuary.

And Planet Earth is
my mother!

CLAY FEET

Like all Earth beings,
I am made of matter.
I eat, drink and breathe
basic elements of Planet Earth
every day.
Planet Earth defines my identity.
Every single day, I eat and excrete
the clay of Planet Earth.

Matter is made from rock and soil;
I am that matter.
Planet Earth pours through me,
replacing each cell in my body every seven years.
I am totally dependent on elements of Earth—
matter is survival:
oxygen to breathe,
moisture to drink,
microbes in the soil
vital for daily bread.

The clay of Planet Earth
is the very ground of my being.

I have the same feet of clay
as every other being on this planet.

I am an Earth being
in search of my roots in Planet Earth—
gravitational,
relational,
spiritual.

EARTH NATURE

I was taught to believe
human beings have souls
and,
according to another dangerous doctrine,
are made in the image of God.

As a human being
I was
superior to all other Earth beings:
endowed by God the Creator
with a capacity to worship,
and a level of consciousness
other Earth beings did not possess.
My being human in God's image
justified
my domination over nature.

Exploring my Earth origins,
I know I have evolved
from a minute organism.

All the impulses
that moved other Earth beings to be
impelled me to become, as I am now:
an Earth being.

From within the mysteries of primal matter
emerged my emotions;
my intellect; my consciousness;
my impulses to love, to empathise,
to explore, to wonder.

Ultimately, my Spiritual awareness
—my sense of the transcendent deep within,
my inner Spirit—
was spawned
by deep impulses of the Spirit in Planet Earth;
the ground of my Earth being nature
lives deep within.

MY FINDING

Earth is my mother;
I am an Earth being
made of clay
and connected to all the mysteries
of nature
by a primal impulse,
a silent Spirit,
deep in Planet Earth
that makes me
delight
in eco-being!

IV

Sacrament of Ochre

SACRAMENT OF OCHRE

On recognising that I am an Earth being
—a child, taken from my mother
by the rite of Baptism
and adopted by Mother Church—
I wonder what kind of ritual could
restore my bond with Mother Earth.

For me, the Sacrament of the Altar
—where Jesus invites us
to drink of the blood that he associates
with a new covenant,
a new treaty,
revoking the old treaty
that Moses made with his God,
a treaty that tolerated no other God,
demanding absolute obedience—
is embedded with deep resonant meaning.

Jesus invites us to bond with him
by drinking blood
and eating bread.
For those at Jesus' table,
blood meant life:
an inner force from a compassionate God
that animates all things,
heals all wounds.

Sacrament of the Ochre:
my name for a ritual celebrated in the Flinders Ranges[3],
when an Adnyamathanha elder invited me,
by marking my skin with ochre,
to bond with Mother Earth.

---

3. In South Australia; Adnyamathanha is the name of the local Aboriginal people who claim this area as their country.

TRADITIONAL RITE

Our Adnyamathanha mentor led us to an ochre pit
in the Northern Flinders Ranges,
a pit with five ochres,
each a different colour,
each with spiritual significance.

The participants encircle
ochre-embedded rocks and the rite begins.
The elder cuts ochre from five locations—
white, gold, red, orange, purple—
crushes each colour into powder,
and cups ochre dust, one colour at a time,
into the palm of one hand.
An assistant trickles water
onto the ochre powder
in the elder's palm
and makes it damp.

The elder dips his thumb into the ochre paste,
marks each participant's skin:
five marks, five coloured ochres,
five symbolic skin sites
on face and neck,
ensuring a spiritual connection
between Mother Earth
and her children.

MARKS

White ochre
links me with the Spirit
in Mother Earth:
the Spiritual force
alive in Planet Earth
and in the ancestors.
White ochre marks my forehead.

Gold ochre
links me with the Sun,
who blesses Planet Earth
who, sun-blessed, becomes
our mother:
source of our personal identity as Earth beings.
Gold ochre marks my cheek.

Red ochre
links me with the life-blood
in Mother Earth—
this inner life-force
stimulates the flow of life
from the womb of Mother Earth.
Red ochre marks my temple.

Orange ochre
links me with the breath of life
rising from the lungs of Mother Earth,
a life-force
that facilitates healing the body
through the lungs.
Orange ochre marks my neck.

Purple ochre
links me with healing forces in the liver,
the symbol of reconciliation and peace
in all relationships.
Purple ochre marks my throat.

RESPONSES

The elder invites participants,
skins marked with ochres
—white, gold, red, orange, purple—
to name the personal spiritual significance
of the ochre rite
for them.

Joining hands, participants
celebrate the Spiritual blessings
from Mother Earth.

For me, the rite was a sacrament,
imparting of spiritual impulses
connected with Planet Earth—
impulses that stirred my inner spirit
affirming my identity as an Earth child.

Later, I began to wonder:
could an Earth-being
Sacrament of Baptism
emerge
from the Sacrament of the Ochre
I experienced in the Flinders?

The ochres
—especially the white ochre—
are symbols of our connection
with the Spiritual in Planet Earth.

My dream:
baptised with white ochre,
I would reconnect spiritually
with my mother, Earth.

WHITE OCHRE BAPTISM[4]

Baptism Elder:
You are invited today
to celebrate a special baptism:
you will receive the mark of white ochre
on your forehead and on your cheeks.
Please take your place around the Earth bowl
where the white ochre is resting
and hear the voice of Earth.

Mother Earth:
Welcome, my Earth children,
to this white ochre baptism.
White ochre is part of me
linked to my inner Spirit,
the mystery of the Spiritual deep within me.
When the elder marks your forehead and cheeks
with white ochre,
you are bonding with me, your Earth Mother,
connecting with kin,
and
celebrating your identity as Earth beings.

Baptism Elder:
I dip my finger in a bowl of water
in a bowl of white ochre.
I mark each of you
on the forehead,
on the cheek,
in the name of Mother Earth.

---

4. A rite created by Earth beings seeking to reconnect spiritually, and to bond with their Earth mother. The ritual needs the following: two celebrants, a bowl of water, a bowl of white ochre.

Mother Earth:
When the elder marks your face,
my children,
with white ochre,
I say to you from my heart:
*Receive the Spirit of Earth
and bond again with me.*

Baptism Elder:
I now invite you to join hands and celebrate your experience together.

Children of Earth:
We celebrate the gift of the Spirit from our Mother.
We celebrate the white ochre blessing
that bonds us with the Spiritual in Mother Earth.
We promise to care for our Mother
as she cares for us.

Baptism Elder:
Let us share the 'Peace of Earth' with each other,
rejoicing in our identity as Earth Beings.

The Peace of Earth be with You!

MY FINDING

*Celebrating
the
Sacrament of the Ochre,
I have a deep consciousness
that I have indeed been baptised again
with white ochre,
and this ritual
represents a new covenant,
bonding me again
with my Mother Earth.*

V

My Cosmic Sanctuary

MICROCOSM

I am an Earth Being;
Planet Earth is my mother.

I explore
my new world,
my new cosmology.

I realise
I am made of clay
like other clay creatures.
I evolved
with a pulse of life
like a platypus.

But Planet Earth. . .
Planet Earth is a mass of mystery,
a panorama of wonders,
a cosmic sanctuary,
a sacred book.

Luther's Planet Earth:
the First Book of God,
embedded
with the mysteries of the universe.

Planet Earth is more
than a book of nature
to read as divine revelation.

Planet Earth is an embryo,
a microcosm of the cosmos;
we can explore the mysteries
of the universe,
and search for the Spirit pulsing,
in a shrine
called Planet Earth.

EARTH'S PULSE

An Earth being,
I know Earth is alive,
pulsing
deep within her core
and across her crust—
a vibrating mass of living matter.

Can I feel the pulse of Earth?
Put my finger on the throbbing extremities?
Connect with the life-forces—
the hidden impulses
of life
that permeate this planet?

If I hold a wild flower in my fingers,
place my hands on the trunk of a tree,
hold the beak of a pelican,
grasp a slippery silver eel,
will I feel the pulse of Earth?

The impulses of Earth
to live,
to sing,
to evoke wonder,
are throbbing in every cell of our planet,
every life-force of Planet Earth,
every scene in the landscape.

I feel the pulse of Earth
with my hands in the air
my feet on the ground
and my Spirit surging,
feeling the throb of life

in every movement,
in every moment,
of my Mother,
Earth.

COSMIC ME

When the space age
burst into my consciousness,
shattering my image of the world,
I became small,
so small:
a insignificant pinprick
on an island
on a planet;
a human footnote
in the never-ending story
of an expanding universe.

An Earth being in Planet Earth,
I awake to the dawn
of the cosmos
breaking through my brain!

I am conscious.
My consciousness:
a climax of the entire cosmos
evolving—
evolving as never before
into the mystery called me.

I am an Earth being;
the mystery of the cosmos
a cosmic consciousness
deep within me
here and now.

MOTHER'S BIRTH

My origins:
the birth of Planet Earth.

Planet Earth:
a piece of stardust,
a minute fragment of galactic matter
spinning through space.

Planet Earth: one
of millions of planets
circling suns,
reflecting light.

Planet Earth: born mysteriously
billions of years ago,
somewhere in space;
an embryo of burning gases
becoming a baby—
becoming Planet Earth.

I do not know
my biological parent's
birth and maturing,
generating water and oxygen
so life evolves and flourishes.

The mysterious deep impulse
enabling all things to be,
to exist and thrive
—everything from black holes in space,
bright butterfly wings,
and the microcosm called Planet Earth—
fascinates me.

Earth beings exist!
I live! We are!
This is amazing!
This is grace!

A cosmic gift reaching back
to the first cosmos impulse—
an impulse we might tag 'capital I';
an impulse whose repercussions
we feel
flowing
through us.
And I am fascinated
that human beings of all ages
intuitively imagine
the mysterious beginnings of Planet Earth.
Human Earth beings share
our deep yearning
to know
our Earth mother's origins.

COSMIC SANCTUARY

Gaze across the night sky,
see the hot spots in space—
blazing balls of gases
exploding superstars and galaxies
speeding through time
with the ferocity of infinity!

What makes Planet Earth unique?
That Earth is a planet,
a fragment of a former fireball?
That Planet Earth
is spinning silently into the distant unknown?
That Planet Earth fends off cosmic rays,
meets meteors, rotates on an unseen axis?

No!

Planet Earth is unique:
Planet Earth is a sanctuary;
a place where life is protected;
a planet permeated by life,
saturated with being.
Planet Earth, our mother Earth, is:
a habitat where humans can survive;
a sacred site in the cosmos;
a cosmic shrine.

Planet Earth is cosmic sanctuary:
a planet kept safe by
an enveloping fragile thin blue line
called atmosphere,
held together by an invisible dark force
in the depths of Planet Earth
called gravity.

Planet Earth is a sanctuary;
we are priests and priestesses,
chosen to sustain and celebrate her mystery
—the mystery of life—
protected in this vulnerable sacred site in the cosmos.

FAMILY

Biology, genetics and evolutionary science
demonstrate we are kin
with all other living things on Planet Earth:
we are all Earth beings.

Some are close relatives;
others are distant kin.
Some are friendly; others are fierce.
All Earth beings are related:
ants, elephants,
sea horses, microbes.

Deep within, human beings share
common genetic codes with all animals;
we all belong to one family:
a diverse community of sentient beings.

Australian Aboriginal Peoples
discern a closeness with nature,
a special kinship with their personal Dreaming:
bird, animal, plant, reptile, fish—
life forms that shared their belonging: their country.

They are conscious of a common spirit
innate within themselves, shared by
their Dreaming kin and located at the sacred sites
of their Dreaming ancestors.

I discern a similar kinship:
a spiritual bond with domains of nature
in tune with my Earth being.

Biologists discern

all beings share a capacity,
an inner impulse
to commune
with other beings,
a deep impulse to connect
with all living things in the universe—
a deep impulse
I celebrate
as an Earth being.

EARTH COMPASSION

Explore the evolution
of our Mother Earth,
and see a battle ground:
the survival of the fiercest in
a 'dog-eat-dog' world.

Sympathise with ecologists
who discern the vital purpose of caring:
the web of compassion
that creates community
in the diverse realms of Planet Earth
and integrates ecosystems.

Planet Earth being generates a caring community,
communicating
—from one species to another—
from the peaks of mountains
to the depths of the oceans.

I sensed a cry in the tsunami
that flooded islands of the Pacific
and inundated the shores of Japan.

The groaning of Planet Earth below
—dangerous dislocations,
not selfish quakings—
sent a message to all creatures.

Some Earth beings—the elephants in Sri Lanka
and the reptiles of Acer—
heard that warning
and fled to higher ground.

Many human Earth beings
were not listening.

They did not hear the warning.

MY FINDING

Earth is my mother—
and so much more:
a cosmic sanctuary
that keeps Earth beings safe;
a compassionate parent
who cares for my kin;
a living habitat
that connects me with the cosmos;
the solar source
of my innate spirit!

VI

My Wisdom Probing

WISE

Following my first discovery
of my hidden nature
via the 'science' of ecology,
I wondered whether, deep in sacred history,
others had discerned that Planet Earth
is a wondrous world
filled with elusive mystery—
not a barren land,
a necessary detour
on our journey to heaven:
our final destination.

I found my answer among the wise:
the scientists of the Wisdom School
in the ancient Near East,
who focused on the observation of nature
rather than revelations
from above.

Their goal:
finding innate Wisdom
by observing the phenomena of nature—
on the ground,
in the skies,
under the oceans,
in society.

Thousands of years later,
I am one of their students,
eagerly pursuing innate Wisdom
in Planet Earth.

INNATE WISDOM

With our focus on acquired wisdom,
we read the Wisdom books,
Proverbs or Job;
learned wisdom from our elders;
from observing human behaviour.

The ancient world wise ones, however,
observed and explored Wisdom
in every realm of nature:
creation's animate and inanimate components
—every one—has an innate 'way'
and a designated 'place' in the cosmos.

The writer of Proverbs tells us to
'observe'
the 'way' of the ant
to get Wisdom!
Every creature
ant, bee, echidna, wombat—
has a 'way':
an innate capacity to be
true to its nature, its essential being.

The Proverbs Wisdom writer declares
four things too amazing to comprehend:
the way of an eagle in the sky,
the way of a snake on a rock
the way of a ship on the high seas
and the way of a man with a maid[5].

As Earth beings, we need to re-view
the dangerous doctrine of original sin;

---

5. Prov 30:18–20.

we need to see the truth of innate Wisdom:
to discern our 'way' is
to discern our profound capacity
to be true to our character,
our true being as Earth Beings—
to be animated
by the Spiritual.

TURTLE WISDOM

Born in the sand
on the Queensland coast of Australia,
a baby sea turtle
scrambles across the beach
impelled by an impulse:
to swim;
swim out to sea
into the deep
alone—
no mother as mentor;
no parent as protector;
to swim
sixteen years
alone,
twenty thousand miles
alone;
to come back home;
to hover ten years more;
to mate;
to lay her eggs,
hoping that, one day,
one baby may reach that shore
wired with an innate Wisdom
no human baby
born alone
on this dangerous beach
could ever
know.

WISDOM EXPERIENCE

Years ago, in Auckland, New Zealand,
sitting on a grassy area
near a shoreline
of a bay,
waiting and watching,
I observed
hundreds of bar-tailed godwits
gathering:
racing around in a feeding frenzy;
communicating extreme agitation.

Suddenly,
heeding a signal deep within,
they began to circle,
forming a spiral of spinning life.
Slowly the spiral swirled out to sea:
godwits setting out across the ocean
—flying across vast waters,
through storms over the equator—
on their way to a chosen location in Siberia,
where they feed, breed,
nurture their young
before they return to Auckland,
New Zealand.

At that moment I could
sense their innate Wisdom
—the Wisdom of flight; the Wisdom of memory—
encoded in their spirits.
I discerned an amazing intelligence
of fellow Earth beings,
guiding themselves non-stop
to a place

across the ocean
more than ten thousand kilometres away!

As they vanished into the distance
I had sense of sheer wonder.

I had discerned Wisdom in nature:
the innate force
driving their evolution
over millions of years.

GOD'S SEARCH

There is a challenging chapter
in the Book of Job[6]:
a Wisdom Manifesto,
where God is portrayed a one of the wise
searching
for Wisdom.

The eternal question remains—
even for God:
'Where can Wisdom be found?'

God searches as a true scientist
across every inch of Planet Earth,
observes everything under the heavens
to discern and find
the 'way',
the 'place',
of Wisdom.

Where does God find Wisdom?
In God's self?

No!

God, the scientist,
observes Wisdom as an innate force
governing the forces of nature.
Wisdom in the innate impulse of the wind!
Wisdom in the vast expanse of the waters!
Wisdom in the 'way' of lightning and thunder!

Where can Wisdom be found?

---

6. Job 28.

In the innate capacity
of the components of Planet Earth
to be true to their inner nature—
whether they be Earth plates,
earthquakes
or
grains of sand!

COSMIC BLUEPRINT

God's special relationship with Wisdom
reflected in Proverbs 8:
the voice of Wisdom declares
YHWH acquired me first,
his way before his works[7].

This declaration challenged me for years:
Wisdom preceding creation;
God 'acquiring' Wisdom—
the necessary design
for creation.

Wisdom claiming to be
the blueprint for creation:
the innate force
guaranteeing the
design,
character,
function,
of all creation
—everything—
from the Big Bang
to the tiniest touch
facilitating
the origins of life.

Wisdom is tantamount
to the innate Spirituality
that determines
the character,
the 'way,'
of the entire cosmos.

---

7. Prov 8:22.

As an Earth being
I am also a feature
—however minimal—
of the cosmic blueprint:
the innate Spirituality
of the
cosmos.

MY FINDING

Wisdom is
a dimension of innate spirituality;
a primordial blueprint
that determines the 'way',
the character
of all in creation—
including
black holes,
Planet Earth,
Earth beings like you and me,
and
shrieking cockatoos.

VII

My Journey with Job

'PATIENCE' OF JOB

As a child, I was told about
a model of piety:
the 'patience' of Job.

One day
our weather-board home
was burned down:
nothing remained, except
a heap of smoking ash.

People driving past our farm
stopped to look
and offer sympathy.
The Lutheran pastor arrived,
placed his hand on my shoulder, and said:
The Lord giveth and the Lord taketh away.
Blessed be the name of the Lord.

Those pious words
made me feel like
punching
the pastor
in the gut.

Job's words
rang in my ears for years
—until I chose to take the journey
from extreme trauma
to Wisdom therapy
with Job.

I realise,
as an Earth being
in tune with the poet–author,
that Job's words
are trauma denial:
the starting point
of my daring
journey.

CORRUPT CLAY BEING

Job's friends were bent
on finding him guilty:
a human being who
deserved divine punishment.

The first of his friends claimed
a frightening revelation:
Job was a clay creature,
an Earth being;
all humans made of clay
are necessarily
corrupt
from birth[8].

This friend claimed
to know God
does not trust angels—
so how could mortals possibly be
inherently righteous
before God.

This ancient version
of the dangerous doctrine
of original sin
challenged me:
follow the
spiritual journey of Job
and reconsider
the nature of human beings
as Earth beings—
in the light of
Job's experience.

8. See Job 4:12–19.

Would Job accept that he was
corrupt clay?

Never!

IMAGE OF GOD?

Job explores what it means
to be an Earth being—
his tragic condition is
overwhelmed by trauma[9].

With a bitter spirit Job declares:
mortals are forced
to labour on Planet Earth,
like slaves longing for wages;
God is a Seeing Eye,
spying on these helpless hirelings
from above.

Job claims his nights are
filled with suicidal
nightmares.

In a sarcastic tirade,
he berates the classic belief
that humans reflect
the image of God.

In the experience of Job,
humans are Earth creatures:
images of slaves
not
images of God.

At this point in Job's journey,
he discerns that
the only true hope of humans
—living images of slaves—

---

9. See Job 7.

to escape the Seeing Eye
is to return to the dust
from which Adam was made.

SCREAM 'BLOODY MURDER', EARTH[10]

Job screams at God numerous times
for terrorising him
with cruel pains and torments,
and poisonous arrows.

Job claims that God
pierces his kidneys without mercy,
and spills his bile on the ground,
even though he is pure,
without any violence in his hands.
Job sees his treatment
as tantamount to
murder at the hands of God.

He calls on Planet Earth
to not cover his blood;
to shout 'bloody murder'—
just as Earth,
tasting the blood of Abel,
screamed.

Job's hope:
someone in heaven, hearing
Planet Earth screaming,
will testify before God
on Job's behalf.

Job refers to Planet Earth
as his mother,
from whose womb he emerged,
naked.

---

10. See Job 16:18–21.

Planet Earth,
not a celestial deity,
is Job's final hope.

I am an aged Earth being
living on Planet Earth;
Job's hope
resonates in me.

WISDOM GOD

There are several different gods
in the book of Job:
the celestial deity
who wagers with the Satan
about the faithfulness of Job;
the friends' righteous God
who rewards good and punishes evil;
the Seeing Eye
who watches Job
to make his life miserable.

Then, in a surprise move:
Job's poet-cum-narrator introduces
God the scientist[11]
who searches and probes
everything on and in Planet Earth
seeking Wisdom.

And this primal Wisdom scientist
observes and discerns Wisdom
as an innate force
in the many realms of Planet Earth—
the Spiritual alive in the laws of nature.

For our Wisdom God
—and for me—
Planet Earth is more than a lump of clay;
Planet Earth is a dynamic world.

---

11. See Job 28.

WISDOM THERAPIST

My close reading of the famous voice
from the whirlwind[12] reveals
God the Wisdom Scientist
is also God the Wisdom therapist.

The voice doesn't challenge
Job's accusations of divine injustice
or Job's claim to be an innocent
subjected to trauma.

The divine therapist challenges Job
to answer a plethora of questions about
the design of the universe;
the Wisdom blueprint of the cosmos;
the operation of Wisdom forces
innate in the realms of Planet Earth and sky.

God the Wisdom Therapist
invites Job, as a travel companion on a trip
to the primordial world,
to witness Earth's construction,
the seas being contained,
and the design of the cosmos.

Job gains cosmic consciousness;
an awareness of why he exists, his place,
who he is: an Earth being
in a world of innate Wisdom mysteries.

I welcome
the Wisdom Therapist
into my life

---

12. See Job 38.

as I probe innate Wisdom
in the design of the cosmos,
especially in
Planet Earth.

COSMIC JOURNEY

I journey through the cosmos
with Job and the Wisdom therapist[13].
I am astounded:
my understanding of ecology
and ancient Wisdom
are deeply interrelated.

I follow Job and the Wisdom therapist
back to the origins of Planet Earth,
the depths of the underworld
and the designated 'places' of light and darkness.
I am amazed as I discern,
in response to the therapist's question,
how the laws of space—
the Wisdom forces in the skies—
establish order on Planet Earth.

Planet Earth is connected
astrologically and ecologically:
laws of space
establish Earth's unique way.
Earth: a living eco-system.

And I, as an Earth being,
am interconnected with space:
the Wisdom laws of the universe.

I am an Earth being:
a human on Planet Earth
with cosmic eco-consciousness
and land consciousness.

---

13. See Job 38:31–33.

MOMENT OF TRUTH

After his long journey
through the cosmos,
and the world of the wild,
Job declares he will not pursue his case against God:
he will leave behind his dust and ashes,
his devastating trauma location[14].

Why?
Because, Job says, 'my eyes have seen God'.

Amazing!
In viewing the domains of the cosmos
—specifically,
discerning innate Wisdom forces
governing these realms—
Job claims to 'see' God.

Realising 'seeing'
is a technical Wisdom School term
for 'observing' a phenomenon of nature,
we recognise Job's comment is
not poetic idiom,
not pious metaphor.

Job discovers
God is not a being
harassing him from heaven.
Job observes innate Wisdom forces
operating in each realm of the universe:
God is the Spiritual
present in the cosmos!

---

14. See Job 42:1–6.

An Earth being
part of the cosmos,
I discern the Spiritual
in all nature's diverse Wisdom forces
in this cosmic sanctuary,
Planet Earth.

MY FINDING

My journey with Job
through the cosmos
moves me
to discover that 'God' is not
a heavy-handed celestial being.
God is the innate spirituality
permeating the cosmos
and evident in the innate Wisdom
that governs Planet Earth.

VIII

My Country

CHALLENGE

Today,
as red gums waver in the wind,
koalas finds comfortable crevices
and
the horizon beckons in the distance,
I reflect on the Spirit consciousness
that I now discern:
my debt to my Aboriginal elders;
my deep probing of my biblical heritage;
my acute awareness of the innate Spirit
calling me from the 'true faith'
back to my country,
the land itself.

I remember words
spoken by Rainbow Spirit elders.

This land is a living place
made up of sky, clouds, rivers, trees,
the wind, the sand;
and the Spirit has placed
my own spirit there, in my own country.
It is something—
and yet it is not a thing
—it is a living entity.
It belongs to me;
I belong to it.
I rest in it.
I come from there[15].

My spirit is in this land,
my country.

15. Rainbow Spirit Elders, *Rainbow Spirit Theology*, 31.

The Spiritual reaches out to me.
I find passion and peace.

PRIMAL PRESENCE[16]

I am sitting
in a crevice of nature.

Stillness,
shimmering stillness.
No wind or wave stirs the stillness.

A feeling of Presence:
intense,
close.

Nature's drives are suspended;
nothing moves.
I can feel nature's primal pulse.

I am suspended—framed in stillness;
captured by Presence.

Sounds hover in the stillness:
a lamb bleats in the distance;
the voice of a fisherman, out at sea, rolls in.

A soft voice in the stillness—hovering, suspended!
Then silence in the stillness.

Is this the moment Elijah knew
in that cave on God's mountain?

God is
not in the storm,
not in the earthquake,
not in the bushfire.

16. A cove on Kangaroo Island, 3 October 2009.

God is
a silent voice
in the stillness.

My innate Spirit is sensitive to Presence,
the Presence in Planet Earth:
innate Wisdom in the realms of Planet Earth.

The Spirit of Planet Earth
whispers to me
in the stillness.

ROCK

I stand on a hill at sunset
overlooking a massive rock;
a mile high, some say,
and twenty miles around.

The rock is Uluru[17],
a golden boulder rising from deep
in the red centre of Australia;
a sacred site for our Aboriginal Peoples.

As I watch,
wonder surges within me—
Uluru changes colour, instant to instant,
from celestial gold to earthy orange,
from vivid bronze to blazing red,
and rich purple:
all the colours of the desert rainbow.

I sense what many have sensed
before me:
that point of Spiritual concentration—
the navel of Planet Earth;
in this place, Uluru,
Spirit incarnate in rock
reveals the intrinsic worth
of Planet Earth.

I sense
my innate Spirit stirring
wonder within me,

---

17. Also known as Ayers rock; a monolith in Central Australia; considered by some as an example of an omphalos: a central point from which terrestrial life originated.

connecting me spiritually
with an ancient sacred site
on Planet Earth.

SACRED CAVE

I sat with Rainbow Spirit elders;
we talked together, read together, wrote together,
and listened to the land together.
They taught me to listen to country,
to be kin with the land,
to be a local Earth being.

I walked with Willie,
a Rainbow Spirit elder;
we visited sacred caves near Cooktown:
here local Aborigines were born;
their bones buried, here, when they died.

I saw where women sat to give birth,
where they buried the afterbirth,
connecting with the Rainbow Spirit
in Planet Earth below.

I saw an image of the Rainbow Spirit,
on the cave wall—
a Presence without a face:
a Spirit stirring my consciousness.

In that cave,
I sensed
that I was
born of Mother Earth,
kin with all Earth beings
in Australia,
and
connected with the
Spirit of country.

LAND AND COUNTRY[18]

When I was privileged to conduct a workshop
with Rainbow Spirit elders,
I re-viewed my accustomed worldview:
western dualism—
soul/body, heaven/Earth. . .

In that shared space,
guided by my Aboriginal mentor,
George Rosendale,
I realised that land is a reality
with deep Spiritual dimensions
I had never imagined.

One of the Rainbow Spirit elders
revealed the
deep spiritual interrelationship
between
elders and land, country.

In each Aboriginal person
there is land and Spirit.
Both of these link each one of us
with the land
and the Creator Spirit in the land.
For us Aboriginal People
to know our true identity,
it is vital for us to know
the specific place in the land
where we belong[19].

---

18. Workshop in Townsville, Queensland.
19. Rainbow Spirit Elders, *Rainbow Spirit Theology*, 62.

I now discern
within me
land and Spirit.

I am an Earth being
made of land and Spirit.

LAND AND LIFE

In Psalm 104,
the biblical tradition links
Spirit and land:
the Creator Spirit
is revealed as the source of life
for the land
and all creatures of the land.

When you turn away
they are afraid,
When you take away your breath
they die
and go back to the dust
from which they came.
When you give them breath
they are created
and you give new life
to the land[20].

The breath of the Creator Spirit
is the Spirit who
animates all life
and the land.

The Rainbow Spirit Elders know
that the Creator Spirit
animates the land
and
imparts a Spirit
to the land itself
and
to all land beings
on Planet Earth—
including me.

---

20. Ps 104:29–30.

ORIGINAL SANCTUS

Over the years
we have sung the
Sanctus at celebrations
of the Eucharist:
Holy, holy, holy,
Lord God of hosts
Heaven and Earth are
full of thy glory.

A close reading reveals
the following:
The whole Earth is filled with
Presence.

Just as Mount Sinai
was 'covered in Presence'
and
the tabernacle was
'filled with Presence',
the Seraphim declare:
The whole of Earth
is filled with Presence.

In the light of our insights
about Planet Earth,
we are invited to celebrate
using the original Sanctus.

Holy! Holy! Holy!
Lord God of hosts.
The whole Earth is filled
with Presence!

MY FINDING

If I dare to listen
to Earth
and to the voices of
my Aboriginal mentors,
I am ready to recognise
and celebrate
a new consciousness—
a land consciousness:
land as a realm
that is not only spiritual
but also deeply personal
and filled with Presence.

IX

My Innate Spirituality

INNATE SPIRIT

Each Earth being
has an innate Spirit—
a deep spiritual impulse
that stirs a distinctive
character in its being—
inherited from Mother Earth.

To call
our innate Spirit
'soul'
is misleading:
soul is often understood
as a separate entity
located
temporarily
in the
body.

Our Earth-being Spirit
is innate;
an integral life-force:
born of Planet Earth;
binding us to Planet Earth,
our geological,
ecological,
Spiritual mother;
source of our eco-Spirituality
as children of
Mother Earth.

WONDER

I wondered
about wonder
and the wonders
of nature.

I realise
my innate Spirit stirs
my experiences of
wonder
and
amazement.

Wonder arises:
facing a blazing rock
like Uluru
or
feeling the delicate fronds
of a
blue wren's
feather.

Wonder is
more than
intellectual interest,
more than
unexpected emotion,
more than
naïve discovery.

Wonder is
the response
of the innate Spirit of an Earth being
to special moments when

Planet Earth connects with us,
her children;
reveals her stunning Presence,
her innate Wisdom,
her close relationship,
with us,
her children.

To wonder is
to listen to Spirit deep within,
to sense the sacred Presence of country,
to hear the silence song
of mystery.

AWAKENING

If I wake in the morning
feeling flat,
like my dog on the mat,
does that mean my innate Spirit
in not really here?

If I contemplate the horizon
in a mental haze
like the mist on the ocean,
does that mean my innate Spirit
is but a dizzy dream
in my poetic soul?

Does that mean
a night of distracting images
from a confused dream world
have blocked
the rise of my Spirit in its home,
its innate habitat
inside me?

Does that mean
demands of the coming day
smother the breath of my Spirit
and force it to retreat
into my deep?

A cup of coffee may not do
the trick—
nor a glass of red wine!

The Spirit within,
I discern,

listens to the Spirit without:
the innate Spirit
in the realms of Planet Earth,
in the rumbling of a thunder storm,
in the greeting of a blue wren,
in the laughing of a kookaburra
in a blazing sunset scorching the horizon.

My spirit awakes
when it senses
the innate Spirits of
Planet Earth
awake.

IMPULSE

At home with Planet Earth
I am aware of two deep spiritual forces:
an initiating impulse;
a permeating Presence.

I discover new impulses
in Planet Earth,
spawned by
deep initiating impulses:
to evolve and explore,
to dance and dine,
to mate and nurture,
to commune and connect,
to celebrate and empathise.

I am
surrounded by
amazing impulses,
in a billion blossoming ways.

I am aware of Presence
in Planet Earth—
deep permeating Presence:
of alluring heights and horizons,
of sacred sites and ecosystems,
of silent mystery in hidden habitats,
of the Spirit of Planet Earth
revealed in stillness.

At home with Planet Earth
I am acutely aware
Planet Earth is here,
with me.

My adoptive Lutheran family
call the initiating impulse
God the Creator,
the permeating presence
the Holy Spirit.

My Mother Earth
names them
Innate Wisdom.

SOUL

In the sixties, my poetry sessions
with Lutheran youth in America
included extemporary poetry.
Challenging the audience to give me a topic,
I would plot a poem
on the spot.

A cluster of black students—
laughing, disbelieving, doubting,
at the back, in Dena, Nebraska;
'Soul' challenges one.

The audience is silent,
waiting for my words.

'That painful pit deep within,
where the Spirit cries with pain-filled passion
for brothers and sisters crushed and crucified
by stones thrown
by whites
in the dark of night...'

Lutherans know soul
as that shiny thing
implanted by God in the body—
on Earth, but destined for heaven.

Living in India,
I recognised
Soul
as a form of deep innate empathy
that stirs deep within me:
a spiritual surge

deeper than
kindness,
concern,
Christianity.

Soul is:
an integral dimension of my Earth being;
my innate Spirit as an Earth being,
rising
when fellow Earth beings
are treated as dirt,
as untouchables.

MYSTERY

My innate Spirit is stimulated by mystery:
the question of the origins
of the universe
—or of the multiverse
after multiple big bangs!

Mystery
is more than an
intellectual puzzle
fascinating scientists
and philosophers.

Mystery
is a spiritual conundrum
stirring minds,
stirring Spirits,
stirring the innate Spirits
of humans
across the centuries.

Planet Earth is
a maze of mysteries,
a web of living wonders,
a world of elusive enigmas.

And every enigma
evokes a why!
Why?
Why? Why?

And those whys
are not answered by
mathematics
or magic.

Whys lure the
innate human Spirit
into
the world of the Spiritual,
the Wisdom mysteries
of the cosmos
encountered here,
a microcosm of the cosmos,
a cosmic sanctuary:
Planet Earth.

MY FINDING

*In the context of my former faith
as a child of God,
my acute consciousness
of my innate Spirit,
of my innate spirituality
linking me to my birth in Mother Earth,
might be called
an ecological conversion,
a homecoming,
a new faith.*

*My new faith is
an acute innate awareness
of the Spiritual in Wisdom forces,
Presence,
wonder,
mystery,
Soul.*

*My new faith is
the art of deep listening
to the Spirit within.*

X

My Double Faith

CALL

One night on the farm,
bedridden by local flu,
I sensed a call;
it stirred my inner self,
my innate Spirit.

I believed the call
—a deep Spirit of love for others—
came from Christ.

My Lutheran worldview,
learned from Mother Church,
understood a call as an invitation to serve
my church, my adoptive mother,
as a minister
of the Gospel Lutherans held dear.

That call might have been
a surge of my innate Spirit
reaching out to connect
with the spiritual world
of my planet home.

Indoctrinated by my adoptive mother
to have faith in Christ,
to serve Mother Church,
I could not discern another option.

I could not consider
this call
as a call to serve
my primal mother,
Planet Earth.

TRUE FAITH

For more than fifty years
I advocated the Gospel
for Mother Church,
announcing unequivocally
that I had the true faith:
faith in Jesus, the redeemer
of all humans,
as the only way
to be part of the Spiritual world
called Father, Son, Holy Ghost.

Jews,
Buddhists,
Australian Aborigines
—or peoples of any other faith—
were condemned by God
to life in hell:
they did not possess
true faith.

The more I explored other faiths,
the more I realised
all human beings
possess an innate Spirit:
a deep Spiritual dimension
that moves us to reach outward
and discern in Planet Earth and beyond
a spiritual impulse,
a power,
a Presence.

I claimed true faith.

Were other faiths
—faiths emerging from
innate Spirits in all human beings—
so false they deserved
damnation?

Hell, no!

OTHER FAITH

I am aware:
that I am an Earth being,
that Planet Earth is my mother,
that I possess an innate Spirit
inherited from my mother.

I am alive to my faith within
and the impulse to discern
the spiritual dimensions
of the world around me.

How do I come to terms with
my other faith—
my 'true faith' that enveloped me
for so many years?

Does my ecological conversion
mean I dismiss my other faith
and become an animist?

What are the faith implications
of discovering innate Wisdom
active in forces of nature
on Planet Earth—
and beyond?

Does the Wendish forest family
of my great-grandfather,
accused of 'double faith' in Europe,
provide a Prussian precedent?

Can I be a child of Mother Earth?
And, at the same time,
a child of God in Mother Church?

Can Earth beings,
aware of their innate Earth Spirit,
join with the children of God,
and celebrate the sacrament
together?

CHOICE

The church has been my mother.
I have been a child of God.
I have friends in the family of God.
We have worshipped together,
followed the way of Christ to help people in need,
identified ourselves as Lutherans.

I now face a dilemma.
Do I continue as an Earth child
who has two mothers:
publicly associating with my church family;
privately enjoying my Spiritual bonds
with Planet Earth in Australia?

If I follow this route,
I needn't break with my church family.
I would live a double life:
a public life with my friends in church;
a private life with my kin in creation.

If I confronted my church family
with the reality
—I am a child of Mother Earth
removed from my mother
and adopted into the family of God—
would they say, 'Sorry'?

Some congregations have said 'sorry':
for abusing country;
for tolerating the removal
of stolen generation children
from their Aboriginal mothers.

Dare I imagine the Christian Church in Australia
saying 'sorry' to Mother Earth?

Option one is clear:
hide my double faith,
live two separate lives,
don't upset my friends in the family of God.

Option two is dangerous:
expose my double faith,
be true to my innate Spirit,
be accused of the heresy of my ancestors.

AUSTRALIAN PRECEDENT

Many Aboriginal language groups[21], post-1788[22],
practised a challenging 'double faith'[23]:
becoming Christians and
preserving elements of their traditional faiths.

Many missionaries were adamant:
Aboriginal converts must denounce their traditional beliefs
and affirm only their Christian faith.
Some Aboriginal groups, however,
continued to explore connections
between Christian faith and Aboriginal beliefs.

Rainbow Spirit Elders in Queensland,
in *Rainbow Spirit Theology*[24],
redeem their Aboriginal heritage
through their Christian faith.
In the double faith of these elders,
their Creator Spirit
is identified with the Christian Father God.

In the very beginning, Earth was
formless and empty of life.
The Creator Spirit, in the form of the Rainbow Spirit,
shaped the land, its mountains, seas, rivers and trees...
From the beginning,
the Rainbow Spirit has been and still is present
deep within the land...

21. Aboriginal people are linked by language, kinship, country, Spirit ancestor, clan/tribe; language group is a significant link between people and place, country.

22. 1788: first Christians arrived in Australia.

23. See poems on pp. [x-ref] for additional nuances of 'double faith'.

24. I edited this book, following conversations with this group of Aboriginal elders.

*This Creator Spirit is known to Aboriginal Australians
by many names, including Yiirmbal, Biame, Rainbow Spirit
and in Christian times, Father God...*[25]

Today, some Aboriginal leaders,
exploring the interrelationship between
Aboriginal and Christian Spirituality,
speak of a two-way faith.

Do my Aboriginal elders provide a precedent
for celebrating a double faith?
Yes!

---

25. Rainbow Spirit Elders. *Rainbow Spirit Theology*, 29–31.

BIBLICAL PRECEDENT

The Aboriginal precedent I describe
has a forerunner
in the New Testament:
in the book of Colossians.

The community in Colossae
was Stoic;
the innate Spiritual force,
logos:
initiating,
animating,
permeating
every cosmic domain.

In the letter to the Colossians,
the writer does not tell
Christian converts
to abandon their Stoic worldview;
the writer invites them to recognise that
Christ
is the *logos*
present
throughout the cosmos.

The Stoics said, *logos* is in all things!
The letter to the Colossians says,
Christ is in all things!

Can I say:
in Planet Earth
logos,
Christos,
the innate Spirit,

the Rainbow Spirit,
is in all things?

Why not?

TWO WAYS

Some of my Aboriginal friends
speak of a two-way faith,
discerning
dimensions of their Aboriginal Spirituality
consistent with
their Christian faith.

I agree:
double faith means two ways.

The term 'way'
identifies the innate Wisdom;
ancient Wisdom scientists discerned 'way'
determines the character
of all nature's dimensions.

'Way' also identifies the *modus operandi*
of Jesus of Nazareth—
his way with suffering strangers,
traumatised harlots,
lonely lepers,
blind beggars.

The way—
overwhelming compassion of a teacher
willing to love the enemy,
set the captive free—
a way I am committed to follow.

Double faith: double way!
So be it.

MY FINDING

I need to make a choice:
quietly continue with a double faith
having two mothers,
worshipping in church
while celebrating my spiritual bonds
with nature;
or
confront my church mother
with my true identity
and see if she will say 'sorry'
to my Earth Mother
for taking me from my mother;
or
celebrate the innate Spirit
discerned by Earth beings
across numerous cultures—
a Spirit Jesus discerned in all:
lepers,
lunatics,
'unclean ladies'.

Conclusion
My 'Life' Line

MYSTERY CALLED LIFE

Diverse reflections
in these poems
reveal dimensions of
my Earth-being consciousness:
innate Spirituality;
Spiritual links with
country,
Planet Earth,
cosmic mysteries.

My final discovery:
life is
the most amazing Spiritual mystery,
deep deep within,
all around,
challenging everything
I have taken for granted—
dangerous doctrines,
traditional truths,
fossil faiths.

My conclusion:
reflect on 'life',
the deepest Spiritual dimension
of my being,
all beings,
and
of my mother,
Planet Earth.

GIFT OF LIFE

Life is gift,
amazing gift,
sola gratia.

I did not earn my life,
achieve life through great deeds,
mighty works,
publications.

My twin brothers
died at birth,
experiencing a few hours of life;
I have known life
for almost ninety years.

My parents played a role
in bringing me into this world.

My mother said:
life
is a gift of God.

My father said:
life
is one those things
that happen on a farm.

I say:
life is a mystery—
a Spiritual wonder
that
amazes me.

Life is gift
—amazing gift—
sola gratia.

SILENT LIFE

If I take my life,
the search is over.

If I seek to take life
and separate life
from my inner self,
from the heart of my soul,
from the pulsing body life animates,
and examine life
alone,
life eludes me,
remains a silent mystery
within me,
alive in lives
all around me,
challenging me with
silent pulsing Presence.

Is silent life
another metaphor for
Presence,
the ultimate Spirituality
within?

LIFE

I watch in wonder
as a biologist probes,
separates one life-form from another,
one microbe from its mother,
a single cell from a complex mass,
a virus from its habitat.

The wonders of the chemical lab—
identifying minute life-forms;
discerning DNA;
separating cells;
classifying their features—
leave me amazed.

Yet, there is one goal,
that no biologist or botanist,
no genius of the electron microscope
inquiring into the miniscule,
has achieved:
separating life
from the living;
identifying this mystery
that animates the core
and activates the heart
of every being.

Life
remains inseparable
in living beings:
an elusive
mystery.

LIFE FORCES

When I explore the mystery called life,
the silent Presence in all that lives,
I become aware
deep within:
this mystery
is sustained by life forces.

Oxygen inhaled,
vitamins consumed,
or
pulse of the heart:
life forces play a role
in keeping life alive.

Life is a deep Spiritual dimension
within me
and all that lives;
do these life forces
reflect a Spiritual dimension?

Is Planet Earth,
the source of all these life forces?

Is Planet Earth
the Spiritual impulse
for all that lives?

Is Planet Earth's Spirit
supporting life?

LIFE IMPULSES

I can see the evidence of past life
in a fossil, a piece of stone.
The life impulses that animated these creatures,
gave them their character,
their way in the world,
is now absent.

I take a seed
and contemplate its nature.
I am aware of dormant life impulse
deep within the seed.
With water, soil, sunshine
this seed will come alive.
The life impulse specific to this seed
enables it to grow,
sprout leaves,
flower,
produce more seed.

Life impulses guide grape seeds,
gum nuts, broad beans. . .
to assume living forms true to their natures.
Life impulse is not DNA
or genetic code;
life is a mystery
that animates,
activates every
component of living creatures.

The same mystery is in
other living beings: kangaroos,
koalas, country kids.

I can take apart every piece
of a living creature—
from its genes to its glands,
from its brawn to its brain;
I can never locate
the silent life
that animates every creature.

Life is a mystery,
an elusive impulse animating
seeds and soil,
camels and caterpillars.
Life cannot be examined under a microscope.

Life is
that Spiritual dimension
of this planet,
this cosmic Sanctuary,
this shrine called Earth;
it permeates every part of my being.

I am alive
because of the gift of silent life,
the Spiritual Presence within me.

My double faith
is silent life:
a spiritual mystery
that one day, in the bush,
I might know as Creator Spirit;
that on another day,
on the beach,
I might know as cosmic Christ.

PRESENCE

Life
may be invisible to the naked eye,
but life's pulsing spirit
permeates Planet Earth,
with expressions of Presence
in
green leaves of a red gum tree,
bright blossoms of a golden wattle,
long leaps of a wallaby,
slippery swirls of a silver eel,
laughing of a kookaburra.

The omnipresence of life
in all life-forms
leads us
to take life for granted
as we work hard,
play games,
face death.

When we foster
life consciousness,
we are blessed with a spiritual awareness
of a spiritual core
in all that lives,
that moves
and animates our being—
biological,
personal
spiritual—
in this cosmic sanctuary
called Planet Earth.

MY FINDING

At my spiritual core
is a mystery called life,
silent life.
invisible life;
a pulsing Presence
supported by numerous life forces,
surrounded
by millions of living beings
each with a Spiritual core
called life.

What a gift!
What a wonder!
What a life!
What a sanctuary!

Appendix A
Rite of Homecoming

Setting: Participants gather at a site that is sacred for the group, or may become sacred by virtue of this rite of homecoming. At the centre of the site is an Earth bowl: a large earthen vessel, filled with soil in which is located a rosemary bush.

BACKGROUND

Leader: The background to the language and focus of this rite is the analogy of homecoming. The analogy is especially vivid for Australians.

One of the practices in colonial societies was the removal and separation of children from their Aboriginal parents, their traditional 'place', and their spiritual roots. They were relocated in institutions hundreds and often thousands of miles away from their homes. Some were adopted into so-called white families.

All of this was done, it was said, 'for their own good'!

Leader: Some of us in Western Christianity today have a sense that something similar has happened to us. We have been removed and separated from Planet Earth, our biological parent, in a variety of ways.

Through baptism we were adopted into the church, the family of God, and came to view heaven as our true home.

Leader: Those of us who have been separated from Mother Earth are also faced with a long journey home.

Through this rite, we are invited to begin that journey home: to listen to the voice of Mother Earth; to recall Earth memories; to reconnect with our roots; to discover again our kinship with Planet Earth.

INVITATION

(For the Invitation, participants join hands around the Earth bowl at the centre of the celebration.)

Leader: We gather at this site at the invitation of Planet Earth.

People: We come conscious that Planet Earth is present with us.

Leader: Planet Earth invites us to come home and reunite with our Earth mother.

People: We come home to be reconciled and to rejoice.

Leader: We are now aware that Planet Earth is a sacred site in the cosmos, permeated with that Presence we call God, manifesting that Compassion we call Christ, and pulsing with that Life we call Spirit.

People: Holy! Holy! Holy! Planet Earth is filled with Presence!

Leader: We also welcome our family of Earth beings: singing creatures from the forests; dancing creatures from the desert; swirling creatures from the seas.

People: We gather to come home, to know our Mother Earth again,
and receive the blessings of Planet Earth.

CONFESSION

(Three people at various points in the group speak for Planet Earth as preparation for this confession.)

Leader: Before we make our confession, let us hear the voice of Planet Earth, recalling Earth's experience with humans.

The Voice of Earth:

> Why, my human children of the modern world,
> did you lose your sense of wonder,
> and prefer wealth to Wisdom at my expense?
> Why did you treat my body as if it were dead matter
> and slice away my living forests?
>
> Why did you become so cruel:
> you polluted my breath with toxins?
> How did you become so insensitive:
> you destroyed harmless species,
> children I birthed and nourished?
>
> How did you lose your inner awareness
> that you, too, are Earth beings,
> sustained by deep mystery?
>
> Why did you feel the need to mistreat me,
> and commit crimes against creation,
> crimes against your mother?
>
> Or is the problem
> related to your adoption by world religions
> like Christianity

who felt justified in subduing,
harnessing, and abusing me?

People: Earth, our Parent, We are sorry for treating you as dirt, as nothing but lifeless matter, but we long to come home to know you as our mother and love you again.

Leader: Let us hear again the anguish of Mother Earth, the pain she experienced when we were separated from our primal parent by dangerous doctrines of the church.

The Voice of Earth:

How, my human children in the Christian church,
did you get separated from me?

I moulded and nurtured you as vital Earth beings.
You listened to the words of your adoptive family, Mother Church:
God gave you a soul: this is your true identity; you are destined for heaven.

You believed that all I gave you was a fragile body,
a temporary residence for your soul.
But I am your mother: the ground of your very existence;
your source of life, linking you with the mysteries of the cosmos, the deep pulses of the universe.

I invite you to know me,
a planet permeated with Spiritual presence,
embracing sacred compassion
and animated by Spiritual forces.

People: Earth, our Parent, we are sorry: for believing you are nobody; for dismissing your love and compassion.

We long to come home to explore the mysteries of our mother and love you again.

Leader: Let us hear the response of Mother Earth as she welcomes us home and seeks to activate within us a new awareness of who she is and who we are as Earth beings.

The Voice of Earth:

> Welcome home, my children. Welcome home.
>
> I love you now as I have for millennia.
>
> I understand that when you were adopted into the Christian church you were not urged to know me as your mother.
>
> And that is sad. But that worldview can be put in the past, forgiven—but not forgotten.
>
> I am not asking you to reject your adoptive family. I am asking you to love me again, to know me as you knew your adoptive parents.
>
> I am asking you to explore with me a rainbow of mysteries within me, Planet Earth.
>
> I am inviting you back to school, to learn about the Spiritual impulses that permeate this planet you call home.
>
> I am inviting you to celebrate being an Earth being.
>
> Welcome home.

People: Earth, our Parent, what a delight to come back home, and experience your love once again.

> Shalom! Shalom! It is good to be home.

SONG: COME BACK HOME

(Melody: Guide me O Thou Great Jehovah; words © Norman Habel, 2000)

> You who watch the highest heaven,
> wond'ring where God's mansions are.
> You who hope to spot an angel
> spinning like a falling star.
> Earth is calling, Earth is calling:

come back home and rest in me.
Come back home and rest in me.

You who build exotic buildings
taller than the forest tree,
don't you know that all foundations
deep, deep down reside in me.
Earth is calling, Earth is calling:
come back home and live in me.
Come back home and live in me.

You who travel Earth as pilgrims,
dreaming where you'd rather be;
God's own presence fills my body,
I am God's own sanctuary.
Earth is calling, Earth is calling:
come back home to life in me.
Come back home to life in me

You who hope for joys in heaven,
do you know the joys of Earth:
ancient forests filled with singing,
seas that shout when whales give birth?
Earth is calling, Earth is calling:
come back home and sing with me.
Come back home and sing with me.

You who long for bread like manna
falling from the hand of God,
know that Earth provides your water,
precious breath and daily food.
Earth is calling, Earth is calling:
Come back home and dine with me.
Come back home and dine with me.

CELEBRATION OF PLANET EARTH

Leader: Let us celebrate Planet Earth, who she is and what she does.

Let us celebrate the deep impulses of Planet Earth: the Spiritual impulse to be born, to know life, to come into being.

People: We rejoice in the impulse of Planet Earth: to give birth to eggs and elephants; to bring forth life from land and ocean; to evolve molecules and monkeys.

Leader: Yes, we celebrate that deep impulse to birth: an impulse we associate with God, the Creator Spirit.

I now place these seeds in our sacred centre to symbolise Earth's impulse to give birth.

(The leader scatters a handful of seeds in the Earth bowl.)

Leader: Let us celebrate the deep impulses of Planet Earth: the impulse to connect and show compassion.

People: We rejoice in the impulse of Earth: to nurture the young and the wild; to commune through aromas and instincts; to love amid disasters and death.

Leader: Yes, we celebrate that deep impulse to connect: an impulse we associate with Christ, the compassionate One.

I now place this nest of eggs in our centre to symbolise Planet Earth's impulse to show compassion.

(The leader places nest with bird's eggs in the Earth bowl.)

Leader: Let us celebrate the deep impulses of Planet Earth: the impulses to animate lives and to celebrate life.

People: We rejoice in the impulse of Planet Earth: to stir the winds that keep trees alive; to lift those creatures who fly or sing; to revive the spirits of all in the deep.

Leader: Yes, we celebrate that deep impulse to celebrate life, an impulse we associate with the Creator Spirit.

I now place these bright blossoms at our centre to symbolise Planet Earth's impulse to celebrate Life.

(The leader places blossoms in the Earth bowl.)

EARTH READINGS

(At this point participants read texts that reflect insights into what it means to come home to Mother Earth or to be a child of Earth: Earth readings from the Bible; from the reflections in *On Being an Earth Being*; from tradition; from the experience of fellow Earth beings...)

SENSING THE PULSE

Leader: You are invited to take a piece of rosemary from the bowl at the centre of our sacred space in preparation for stimulating our senses as we seek to reconnect with Planet Earth.

(Participants move to the earthen bowl at the centre, take a piece of rosemary and return to their place; this is an opportunity for quiet reflection.)

Leader: We re-connect through sight.

We focus our eyes on the rosemary in our hands: its shape, its colour, its inner power—the living impulse that causes a plant to emerge from Planet Earth.

(Participants focus their eyes briefly on the rosemary in their hand.)

People: Mother Earth, help us to sense the silent impulse within this rosemary that brings this plant to life in this distinctive form here and now.

Leader: We re-connect through hearing.

We brush the rosemary across an ear and hear the sound— the song it makes as it touches our skin, our mind, our Spirit.

(Participants brush the rosemary back and forth over their ear.)

People: Planet Earth, help us to hear the deep impulse within, continually breathing life into us and all the plants on this planet.

Leader: We re-connect through touch.

We feel the rosemary between our fingers: its texture, its skin, its rough stem—a life made from Earth.

(Participants feel the texture of the rosemary between their fingers.)

People: Planet Earth, help us to discern the hidden impulse within: the Wisdom implanted in this plant; the mystery that makes rosemary rosemary.

Leader: We re-connect through smell.

We crush a few leaves of rosemary and smell its soul: the aroma from a plant that penetrates our inner selves.

(Participants crush a few leaves and smell the rosemary.)

People: Planet Earth, help us, through this aroma, to sense rosemary as a symbol of Presence that evokes mystery among us.

Leader: We re-connect through taste.

We take a few leaves of crushed rosemary and taste them: savour the rich herb flavour—a gourmet gift to celebrate Life.

(Participants taste and savour a few rosemary leaves.)

People: Planet Earth, help us to: celebrate this plant; celebrate all Earth life; celebrate life as it pulses through us.

EARTH MEMORIES

Leader: Rosemary is a symbol of remembering.

In this time and place, as we come home to Mother Earth, we are invited to focus on early memories of our bond with Planet Earth.

The first memories you are invited to recall are Planet Earth memories from your early childhood. When did you feel close to Mother Earth as a child? Did you feel a kinship with trees, animals or some other part of the Earth community?

You are invited to share these Earth memories as offerings of thanks.

(Participants share their childhood Earth memories, write them down and bring them to the centre.)

Leader: You are now invited to share memories of Earth consciousness: those moments, times or experiences when you had a strong sense of the life impulses in Earth. Did you feel that you were indeed an Earth being?

You are invited to share these memories as an expression of faith.

(Participants share their memories of Earth consciousness, write them down and bring them to the centre.)

Leader: Mother Earth, we return to you the memories you have given us.

People: Planet Earth, we thank you for stirring our memories, for helping us re-connect with you, for welcoming us home.

SONG: MOTHER EARTH

(Melody: Praise my Soul the King of Heaven; words © Norman Habel, 1999)

Mother Earth, our mother birthing
ev'ry creature from the ground;
Jesus too was flesh and breathing,
kin to all that's green and brown.
Celebrate with all creation:
find God in the web of Life.

Sister Air, our sister lifting
ev'ry creature born with wing;
Jesus shared the breath of forests,
breath that makes our spirits sing.
Celebrate with all creation:
join God in the song of Life.

Brother Water, brother pulsing
deep through ev'ry vein and sea,
Jesus drank the very raindrops
in our wine and in our tea.
Celebrate with all creation:
toast God in the feast of Life.

Father Fire, our father burning
with the sacred urge to move,
help the Spirit of this planet
stir our inner selves to love.
Celebrate with all creation:
feel God in the pulse of Life.

BLESSING

Leader: May your pulse be one with the pulse of Planet Earth, the silent Life deep within all creation.

May your voice join the voices of Planet Earth in songs of celebration!

May your deep self bond anew with Mother Earth, your first parent.

May your spirit groan with the Spirit groaning in creation.

May your heart find in Planet Earth the Wisdom to fulfil your way in Life!

May you learn from Planet Earth how to serve rather than dominate your kin!

May Planet Earth reveal to you the Spiritual Presence, the life throbbing in, with and under all creation!

People: Shalom! Shalom!

It's great to be home.

(Participants greet each other with a greeting of peace: Shalom! Shalom! They may also greet their immediate environment, the Earth site where they are located, with the same words.)

Appendix B
Workshop: Exploring Earth Spirituality

PREFACE

This workshop is based on the reflections about Being an Earth Being found in *On Being and Earth Being: Exploring the Spiritual in a Cosmic Sanctuary Called Planet Earth.*

The goal is for you as participants to explore the insights and challenges articulated in the various chapters of this volume, to discuss the spiritual relationships with Planet Earth that you have discovered, to celebrate a relevant Earth ritual and to reformulate your findings in personal diaries.

SUGGESTED FORMAT FOR THE WORKSHOP:

Introduction by the workshop leader outlining the plan for the three-session workshop. Each session will include:

- Presentation
- Readings
- Explorations
- Rite of Celebration
- Diary of Findings

SESSION 1

Presentation: Earth Identity and Earth Spirituality

Readings: selected reflections from chapters 1–3: Adoption, Heritage, Earth Identity

Explorations:

- What do you think happened when you were baptised? How do you feel about the suggestion that you were adopted through baptism, purged of original sin and made a child of God destined for your home in heaven?
- How do you respond to the idea that Earth is your true mother, the very source of your origin and identity? Have you ever felt this sense of connection with Planet Earth?
- How do you interpret the story of the Fall in Genesis 2–3?
- Do you ever relate to Earth as a spiritual domain filled with the breath or presence of God? When? In what context?
- What does Psalm 139.13–15 say about your origin?
- How has ecology given you a deeper consciousness of your identity as an Earth being and of Earth Spirituality?

Celebration: White Ochre Baptism (see chapter 4)

Diary of Findings about:

- Baptism
- Being an Earth Being
- The story of the Fall
- Ecology
- Earth spirituality

SESSION 2

Presentation: Cosmic Sanctuary and Innate Wisdom

Readings: selected reflections from chapters 5–8: Cosmic Sanctuary, Wisdom Probing, My Journey with Job.

Explorations:

- What does understanding that you are linked to the origins of Planet Earth as a component of the cosmos mean? How would you celebrate your cosmic consciousness?
- How does being conscious of the reality that Planet Earth is a Cosmic Sanctuary that keeps us safe affect your understanding of life on Earth? How do you understand the idea 'Earth keeps us safe'?
- What do you know about the ancient Wisdom school of thought in which the wise were tantamount to scientists? How did they function? What did they find?
- What do you understand by the concept 'Innate Wisdom'? What do you discern about the Wisdom innate in ants or the Alps? Or the Wisdom in the clouds?
- What do you understand happened on Job's cosmic journey? Where did he discern Wisdom? What do you understand by Job's comment that he 'sees God?'

Celebration: Earth as Cosmic Sanctuary (see Appendix C)

Diary of Findings about:

- Cosmic consciousness
- Earth as a cosmic sanctuary
- Innate Wisdom
- Job 'seeing God'

SESSION 3

Presentation: Double Faith and Spiritual Presence

Readings: selected reflections from chapters 9–10 and Conclusion: My Innate Spirituality, My Double Faith, My 'Life' Line.

Explorations:

- How do you think exploring the idea that you are not only an Earth being but that you also have an innate Spirit that links you to Earth as your mother and the spiritual centre of the land would change your ideas about yourself and life on Earth?

- How do you think accepting the idea that, among the many mysteries of the cosmos your innate Spirit links you to the innate Wisdom of the cosmos, might change your understandings about who you are?

- Have you explored other faiths, discovered that some of their ideas connect with your own understandings, and find yourself wondering whether you could have a double faith? If you now feel you have double faith as a child of Mother Earth and a child of Mother Church or another traditional faith, what issues and/or challenges does this raise for you?

- If you have ever sought to understand that mystery called 'Life' that hovers silently in all that lives, what did you decide 'being alive' means? If silent 'Life' is another name for Presence or spirituality within you, or within Planet Earth, how does this affect your understanding?

Diary of Findings about:

- Innate Spirituality of Planet Earth
- Dimensions of your own innate spirituality
- Double faith as a child of Mother Earth and a child of God
- Your consciousness of Life as a silent mystery within you and the world of nature

Celebration: Rite of Homecoming (see Appendix A)

Appendix C
Celebrating our Cosmic Sanctuary

BACKGROUND

During the Season of Creation, which is now celebrated in September across the globe, worshippers have celebrated many realms of Planet Earth on Sundays such as Land Sunday, Mountain Sunday and Storm Sunday. On the fourth Sunday of the Wisdom Series (Year C) they have also celebrated Cosmos Sunday. (See the Season of Creation website for details.)

In a special volume entitled *Seven Songs of Creation*, which also relates to the Season of Creation, the series of liturgies begins with Song of Sanctuary, celebrating a song by the same name.

These two modes of celebration with creation highlight rich dimensions of the Cosmos as God's creation and of Earth as a sanctuary embracing God's presence. There is, however, another dimension of Planet Earth that has not been celebrated in these liturgies as a wonder and mystery of our universe.

Planet Earth is not only a sanctuary embracing the divine Presence as Isaiah 6.1–3 testifies, but also a 'cosmic' sanctuary, a planet shrine, a unique locus in the cosmos where life is sustained and protected from the damaging forces in space. Yes, Planet Earth is a sanctuary that keeps us safe.

In the Earth Care Charter I prepared for Lutheran schools, I begin with the challenge: the time has come for us to view Earth as something more than a ball of stardust.

Why?

Because Planet Earth is a haven, a safe place in a dangerous cosmos where amazing forms of life are protected and can flourish.

Because Planet Earth is unique, an oasis in space, where the mystery of Life can be sustained and celebrated.

COSMIC SANCTUARY CELEBRATION
SONG: I'M AN EARTH BEING

(Melody: Morning Has Broken; **words** © *Norman Habel, 2010)*

Born of this planet, I'm an Earth being,
Born of this planet, I'm an Earth child.
One with all beings, born of this planet,
I'm an Earth being, one with the wild.

Born of this planet, baptised with moisture,
I'm an Earth being, blessed by her rains;
Rising from oceans, flowing through rivers,
Earth's sacred waters pulse through my veins.

Born of this planet, flowing with breezes,
Children inhale Earth's infinite breath;
Earth's holy breathing enters my body,
Creating a presence deeper than death.

Born of this planet, one speck of stardust,
We feel the pulsing deep in our soul,
Myst'ry like music throbs in the landscape,
Earth our true mother, makes our life whole.

INVITATION TO CELEBRATE

Leader:
Come enter the Cosmic Sanctuary,
the sanctuary called Planet Earth.

All:
We enter our Cosmic Sanctuary and
celebrate with all that lives in Planet Earth,
with wombats, dingoes and crocodiles,

with golden wattles and old red gums,
with all our kin in this green sanctuary.

Leader:
Come conscious Earth Beings,
celebrate being children of Earth.

All:
We enter our Cosmic Sanctuary,
aware that this planet is also our mother,
the source of our being as children of Earth,
the one who has cared for us every day,
a guardian parent who protects us
and blesses our lives with mercy and love.

Leader:
Come enter our Cosmic Sanctuary
filled with Presence.

All:
We enter our Cosmic Sanctuary
and behold Presence filling the planet,
Presence in the forests,
Presence in the land,
Presence in the oceans
Presence in our Sanctuary.

Leader:
Come and raise your hearts in thanks
for your protection from the dangers of the cosmos.

All:
We enter our Cosmic Sanctuary
conscious that we have been protected
by the mystery of a thin blue line

on the surface of Earth called the atmosphere
and an invisible dark force
in the depths of Earth called gravity.

Leader:
Come celebrate our Cosmic Sanctuary.

All:
Holy! Holy! Holy!
Planet Earth is sacred.
Planet Earth is safe.

READINGS

Reading 1: Prov. 8.22–31
Reading 2: Isaiah 6.1–3
Reading 3: John 1.1–5, 14

VOICES FROM THE READINGS

The Voice of Wisdom:
I am primordial Wisdom
the blueprint employed in the design of the cosmos,
the blueprint that preceded the Big Bang
and implanted innate Wisdom
in all the realms of the cosmos,
to establish their inherent character,
including that of Planet Earth
as a Cosmic Sanctuary.

The Voice of Logos:
I am logos, the cosmic Christ,
the primordial spiritual impulse,
the creator Spirit of the cosmos

that preceded the Tiny Touch,
when I animated the cosmos
and transformed Planet Earth
into a Cosmic Sanctuary
where I sustain and protect Life.

The Voice of Earth:
I am Planet Earth,
a precious piece of stardust
selected to be the mother of Earth Beings
and to become the Cosmic Sanctuary
where spiritual Presence
has permeated the entire natural world
for Earth Beings to see and celebrate.

All:
Holy! Holy! Holy!
Wisdom governs the design of the Cosmos!
Logos sustains Life in the Cosmos!
Presence blesses the Sanctuary of the Cosmos!
Holy! Holy! Holy!

CONFESSION

Leader:
Let us confess how we have treated our Cosmic Sanctuary, a planet filled with Presence.

All:
Alas, we have not treated Planet Earth
as a sanctuary or sacred shrine,
but as a mass of lifeless matter
that can be desecrated by destroying forests,
spreading atomic evils
and violating oceans with pollutants,

thereby upsetting the balance of nature
governed by cosmic Wisdom.

Leader:
Let us confess how we have treated our Cosmic
Sanctuary, a planet protecting our lives.

All:
Alas, we have, in recent years,
pumped harmful greenhouse gases into the air
so that the atmosphere, our protective covering,
has been penetrated
and we have caused the
crisis of a climate change
that damages our Cosmic Sanctuary.

Leader:
Let us promise to relate to our Cosmic
Sanctuary as committed custodians.

All:
We now agree to make a covenant with Earth,
to raise awareness in our respective communities
as to the unique nature of Planet Earth
as a Cosmic Sanctuary
and to find ways of preserving the Sanctuary
that has protected us since Life began.

REFLECTION

(One or more participants may reflect on the readings for the occasion. Or, participants my read with due reverence one or more of the reflections in chapters 5–7 in *On Being and Earth Being*.)

BRAINSTORM

Leader:
Let us now brainstorm in groups and
explore ways in which we might raise
awareness of the special nature of Planet Earth
as a Cosmic Sanctuary and the wounds
that have been inflicted on our planet home
by human behaviour.

(The outcome of these brainstorm sessions may be an agreement to make of covenant with Planet Earth.)

SONG: THE COVENANT WITH EARTH

(Melody: The Lord's my Shepherd; words © Norman Habel, 2011)

We hear the call of planet Earth
to come back home and see
the living presence of our God
in soil and sky and sea.

We hear the call of Mother Earth
to feel her cries of pain,
the way pollution chokes her breath
and toxins burn her brain.

We hear the call of Christ again
to celebrate the news
that Christ, the cosmic mystery,
can heal creation's blues.

For God became a piece of Earth,
incarnate in the Son,
to reconcile a broken world
and make creation one.

We hear the call from deep within
to follow God's own cue
to make a covenant with Earth
and to her soul be true.

And with this covenant we make
a promise bold and free
to heal and care for Mother Earth,
alive with mystery.

CONSCIOUSNESS CREED

Leader:

Let us now, together, declare

our consciousness of our identity

as Earth beings,

our empathy for Mother Earth,

and our appreciation of Planet Earth

as our Cosmic Sanctuary.

All:

We are conscious that we are Earth beings,

and that Earth is the source and sustenance

of our very existence and all our Earth kin.

We are conscious of the empathy we experience

when we sense the suffering and injustice,

inflicted on Planet Mother,

and are moved to follow the way

of Jesus of Nazareth to effect healing.

We are conscious not only that

we have been blessed with the gift of Life,

but also that Planet Earth is also our cosmic Sanctuary,
a shrine that keeps us safe
and blesses us with spiritual Presence.

CLOSING BLESSING

Leader:
As we leave this place
may we become conscious of the blessings
that we receive every day
from within our Cosmic Sanctuary.

May we become increasingly conscious
of the blessings of Wisdom,
the innate force that governs our planet.
All:
Shalom. Shalom.
Wisdom governs our planet.
Leader:
May we become increasingly conscious
of the blessing of Presence,
the spiritual force that permeates our planet.
All:
Shalom! Shalom!
Presence permeates our home.
Leader:
May we become increasingly conscious
of the blessing of Planet Earth,

the cosmic sanctuary that sustains our lives.

All:

Shalom! Shalom!

Earth sustains our lives.

Leader:

Let us close by passing the Peace.

Shalom! Shalom!

Earth is our home!

SONG: COSMIC WISDOM

(Melody: Praise my Soul the King of Heaven; words © Norman Habel, 2014)

Wisdom has a secret message:
do you know where I am found?
Can you find the deepest myst'ry
in the sky or underground?
Listen to the voice of Wisdom
calling us to find her place.

Wisdom is the primal blueprint,
there before the world began,
chosen by a cool Creator
to design the cosmic plan.
Listen to the voice of Wisdom
call before the first big bang.

Wisdom is a silent impulse
hidden deep in nature's law,
guiding wind and cloud and weather,
making ripples on the shore.
Listen to the voice of Wisdom

calling us to feel her pulse.

Wisdom fills the world with wonder,
time and space with wild surprise,
guiding gentle genes through hist'ry,
spinning stars across the skies.
Listen to the voice of Wisdom.
in and under ev'rything.

I am Wisdom, I am wonder,
I was at creation's birth.
Now I'm calling you to listen
to the cries of Baby Earth.
Listen to the voice of Wisdom,
mid-wife of our precious Earth.

Bibliography

Habel, Norman. *The Earthcare Charter and 95 Eco-theses*. Adelaide: Lutheran Education Australia, 2017.

———. *Seven Songs of Creation: Liturgies for Celebrating and Healing Earth*. Cleveland: Pilgrim, 2004.

Habel, Norman, ed. *The Season of Creation, A Preaching Commentary*. Minneapolis: Fortress, 2011.

Rainbow Spirit Elders. *Rainbow Spirit Theology*. Adelaide: ATF Press, 1997.

www.ingramcontent.com/pod-product-compliance
Lightning Source LLC
Chambersburg PA
CBHW051102160426
43193CB00010B/1280